Contents

Some words are printed in bold, **like this**. You can find out what they mean on page 30. You can also look in the box at the bottom of the page where they first appear.

Every king should have one

About 700 or 800 years ago, castles were really important. This time is known as the Middle Ages. Every ruler in the Middle Ages had a castle. Some kings or queens had a lot of castles!

Castles were built to be safe from attack. A ruler could control all the countryside around the castle. A castle was also the ruler's home. **Knights** lived there, too. The knights were trained to fight anyone who attacked the castle.

Life in a castle was hard work unless you were the ruler. Most jobs had to be done by hand. **Simple machines** made some jobs easier. In this book we will learn about simple machines. We will also look at how simple machines were used to build, attack, and protect castles.

Hard work!

Building a castle was hard work! Most jobs were done by hand. Many workers were needed. A castle could take 10 years to build. It might need 2,500 workers.

knight   in history, an important man who was trained to fight

simple machine   tool used to push or pull something

Castle Under Siege!

Andrew Solway

Raintree

www.raintreepublishers.co.uk

Visit our website to find out more information about **Raintree** books.

To order:
☎ Phone 44 (0) 1865 888112
🖹 Send a fax to 44 (0) 1865 314091
💻 Visit the Raintree bookshop at **www.raintreepublishers.co.uk** to browse our catalogue and order online.

First published in Great Britain by Raintree,
Halley Court, Jordan Hill, Oxford OX2 8EJ,
part of Harcourt Education.
Raintree is a registered trademark
of Harcourt Education Ltd.

© Harcourt Education Ltd 2006
First published in paperback in 2007
The moral right of the proprietor has been asserted.

Editorial: Lucy Thunder and Richard Woodham
Design: Michelle Lisseter, Carolyn Gibson, and Kamae Design
Illustrations: Kamae Design
Picture Research: Melissa Allison and Lynda Lines
Production: Camilla Crask

Originated by Dot Gradations
Printed and bound in Europe by Printer Trento

ISBN 1 844 43845 7 (hardback)
10 09 08 07 06
10 9 8 7 6 5 4 3 2 1

ISBN 1 844 43860 0 (paperback)
11 10 09 08 07
10 9 8 7 6 5 4 3 2 1

British Library Cataloguing in Publication Data
Solway, Andrew
Castle Under Siege!: simple machines
621.8
A full catalogue record for this book is available from the British Library.

Acknowledgements

The publishers would like to thank the following for permission to reproduce photographs: AKG Images pp. 15 (left), 28 (top), 29 (bottom); Alamy p. 24 (Pixoi Ltd); Ancient Art & Architecture p. 27; Beatriz and Kurt Dillard p. 12; Bridgeman Art Library p. 23 (Pieter Brueghel/Kunsthistorisches Museeum); Collections p. 20 (Michael Jenner); Corbis pp. 5 (Royalty-free), 11 (Angelo Hornak), 29 (top) (Chris Hellier); DK Images p. 15 (right); England's Medieval Festival p. 19 (Herstmonceux Castle); Rex p. 7 (Paul Cooper); Robert Harding Picture Library p. 8–9.

Cover illustration by Darren Lingard.

Every effort has been made to contact copyright holders of any material reproduced in this book. Any omissions will be rectified in subsequent printings if notice is given to the publishers.

The paper used to print this book comes from sustainable resources.

Disclaimer

▲ *This castle was built in the Middle Ages. It could stand up to an attack by an army.*

Building a castle

Stonemasons were very important. They built the castle's huge stone walls and towers.

A stonemason's most useful tools were **wedges**. Wedges were triangle-shaped pieces of wood. They were thin at one end and wide at the other. Wedges were used to cut stone.

A wedge is a **simple machine**. It turns a downwards push into an outwards push.

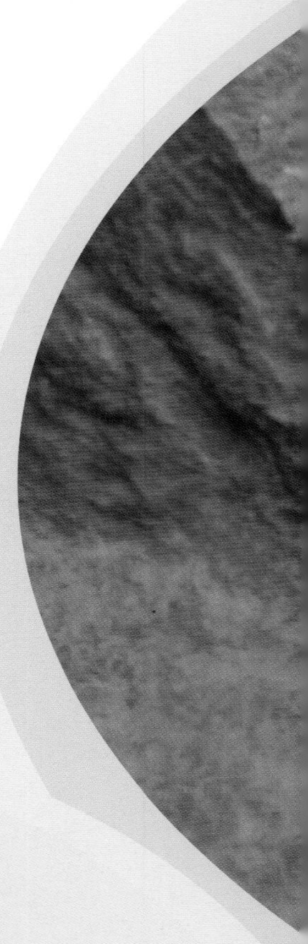

When a wedge is ▼ pushed downwards into a block of stone, it pushes very strongly outwards.

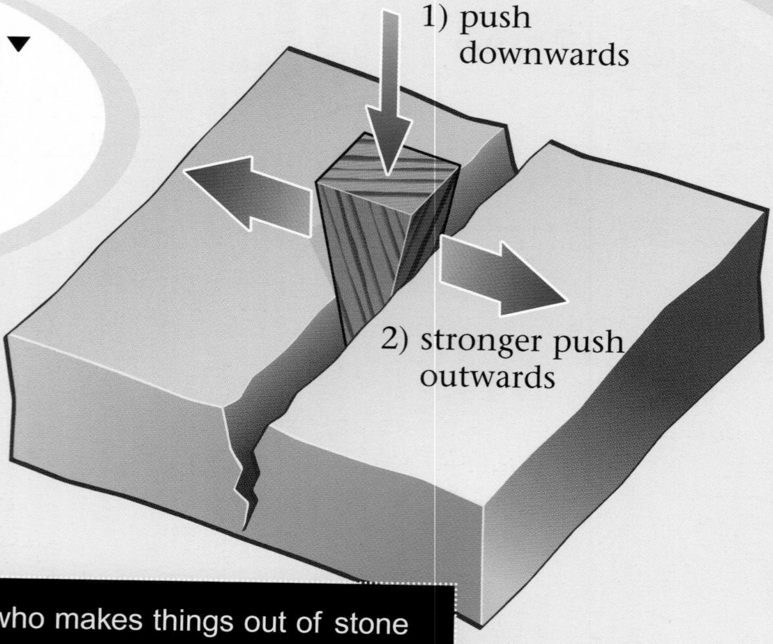

1) push downwards

2) stronger push outwards

stonemason	person who makes things out of stone
wedge	piece of wood or metal that is thin at one end and thick at the other

Stonemasons cut stone ▲
into blocks. They used a
hammer and chisel. A chisel
is a type of wedge.

Moving the stones

The cut stones had to be carried to the castle. They were usually carried in carts. The carts were pulled by horses.

Most castles were built on a hill or high ground. The sloping road leading up to the castle was a **simple machine**. The sloping road was a **ramp**. A ramp has one end higher than the other. Lifting a heavy load is hard work. Moving a heavy load up a ramp is easier. But a load has to travel further when you use a ramp.

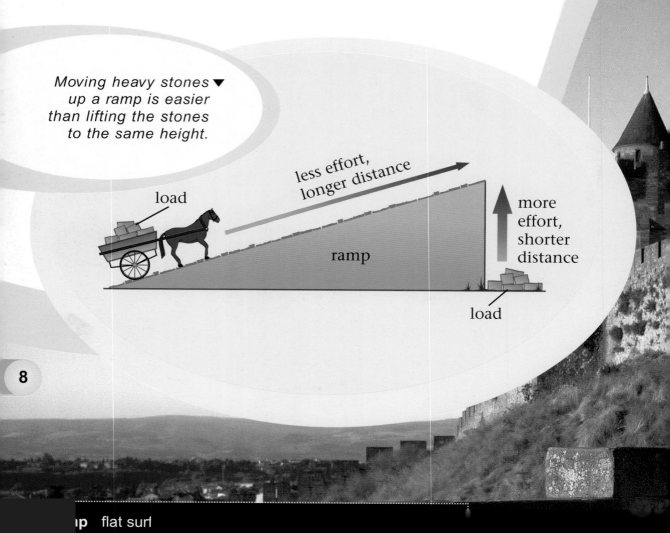

Moving heavy stones ▼ up a ramp is easier than lifting the stones to the same height.

load

less effort, longer distance

more effort, shorter distance

ramp

load

ıp   flat surl

▲ There is a path leading up to this castle. The path is a type of ramp.

Safe from attack?

There were wars in the Middle Ages. Armies often tried to capture enemy castles. This was not easy! Soldiers would usually have to get up a steep hill. They would then have to get over a deep moat (lake). The castle's stone walls were too thick to be knocked down. The soldiers inside the castle could fire arrows at attackers.

One way to capture a castle was to surround it with an army. The army stopped people going in or out. This was called a **siege**.

The people in the castle might run out of food. They might run out of water if the siege lasted a long time. But castles could store enough food to last for months. Most castles also had a well so that they would not run out of water.

A castle is protected from▶ attack in many ways.

siege   when an army surrounds an enemy castle

11

Lifting the drawbridge

So, what actually happened in a **siege**? Usually, the only way into a castle was the drawbridge. If the castle was attacked, the drawbridge was lifted. Then no one could get in.

Most drawbridges worked using two long pieces of wood. These pieces of wood are **levers**. Levers are **simple machines**. Each lever was fixed at a point called the **fulcrum**. The levers moved around the fulcrum.

Soldiers pulled down on one end of the lever. The other end went up. This lifted the drawbridge.

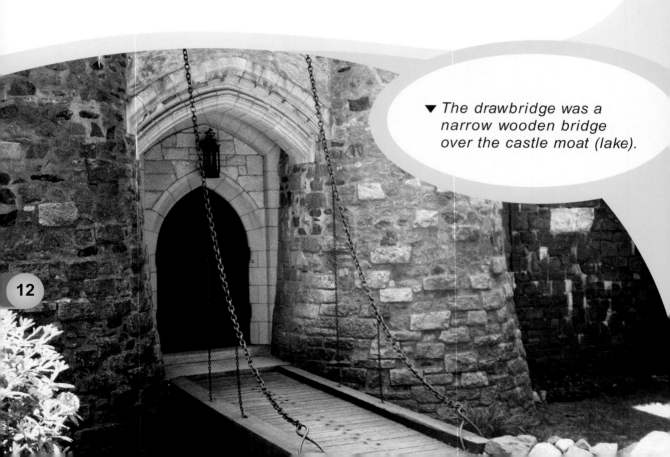

▼ *The drawbridge was a narrow wooden bridge over the castle moat (lake).*

How a drawbridge works

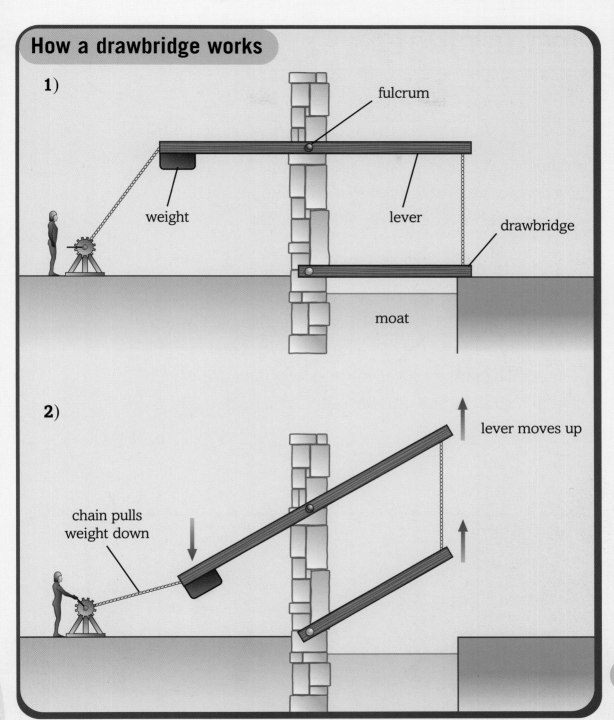

1)

fulcrum

weight

lever

drawbridge

moat

2)

chain pulls
weight down

lever moves up

fulcrum   fixed point that a lever moves around
lever   beam of some kind that can move around
a single point called the fulcrum

Under siege!

In a **siege**, the attackers surrounded the castle. But they didn't get too close. The castle soldiers had crossbows!

Crossbows were deadly weapons. This was because a crossbow was very stiff. It was so stiff that an **archer** could not pull the string back with his hands.

The archer turned a handle to pull back the string. The handle turned a **screw**. A screw is a rod of metal with a spiral cut into it. The string was pulled back when the archer turned the handle. The string wrapped around the screw. The string moves more slowly than if it was pulled in a straight line. But the pull is much stronger.

Make a screw!

A screw is a rod with a **ramp** rolled around it. You can make a screw with a pencil and some paper. Cut a triangle shape out of paper. Starting at the wide end, roll the triangle around a pencil. This is a screw!

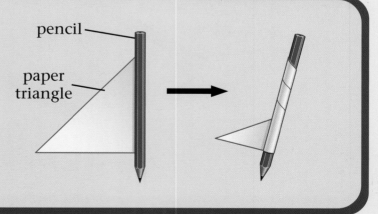

pencil

paper triangle

archer   soldier who uses a bow to fire arrows
screw   rod of wood or metal with a spiral shape around it

screw

▼ *A crossbow from the Middle Ages.*

arrow

handle

This is a different type of ▶ crossbow. The archer is turning the handle to tighten the string.

15

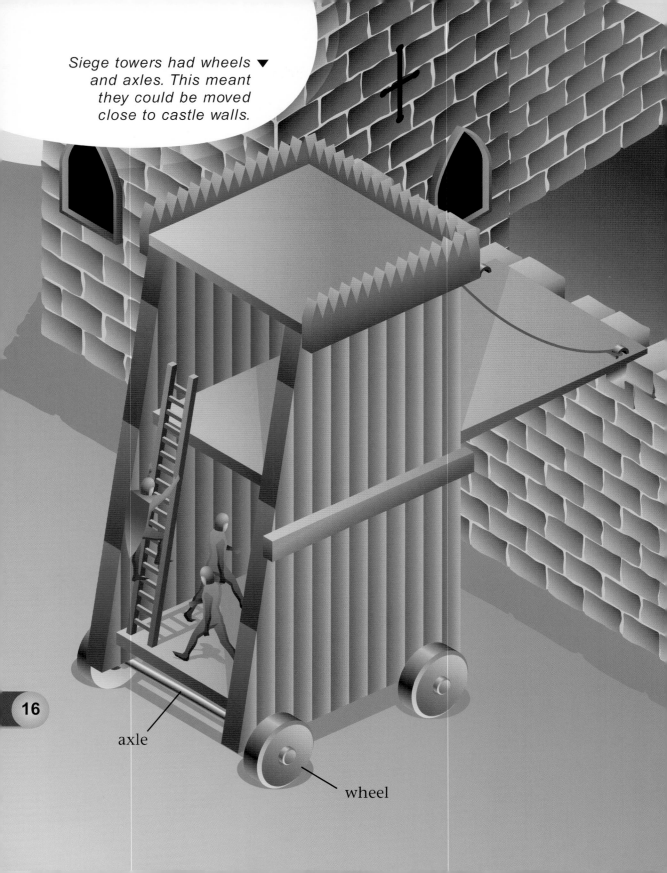

Siege towers had wheels ▼
and axles. This meant
they could be moved
close to castle walls.

axle

wheel

Siege towers

At the start of a **siege**, the surrounding army would often attack the castle. This was to find out if the castle was well protected. One way to attack was to use siege towers. These were tall, wooden towers on wheels.

The attackers pushed the siege towers up to the castle walls. Groups of soldiers stood at the top of each tower. The soldiers then jumped on to the castle walls.

The wheels on the siege tower made it easy to move. The wheels were joined to **axles**. An axle is a rod with a wheel at each end.

A wheel and an axle make a **simple machine**. It is much easier to move a heavy load on wheels than to drag it over the ground.

axle   bar with a wheel or wheels joined to it

Giant catapults

If the **siege** did not work, the attackers could try to break the castle walls. They used giant catapults to break the castle walls. Catapults could throw large stones at high speed.

A giant catapult used a **lever** to throw a stone. The lever was a long beam. It was fixed at a point called the **fulcrum**. On one end of the lever was a very heavy weight. On the other end was a strong band of material. This was called a sling.

Soldiers put a stone inside the sling. They used ropes to pull down the sling end of the lever. The lever was held down with a large pin. When the pin was pulled out, the heavy weight crashed down. This made the sling end of the lever fly up very quickly. The stone was thrown towards the castle.

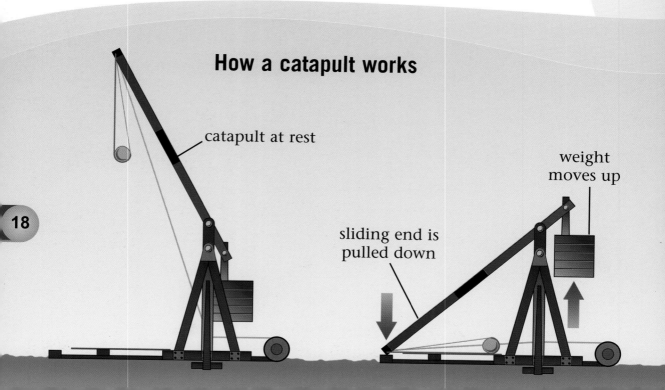

How a catapult works

catapult at rest

sliding end is pulled down

weight moves up

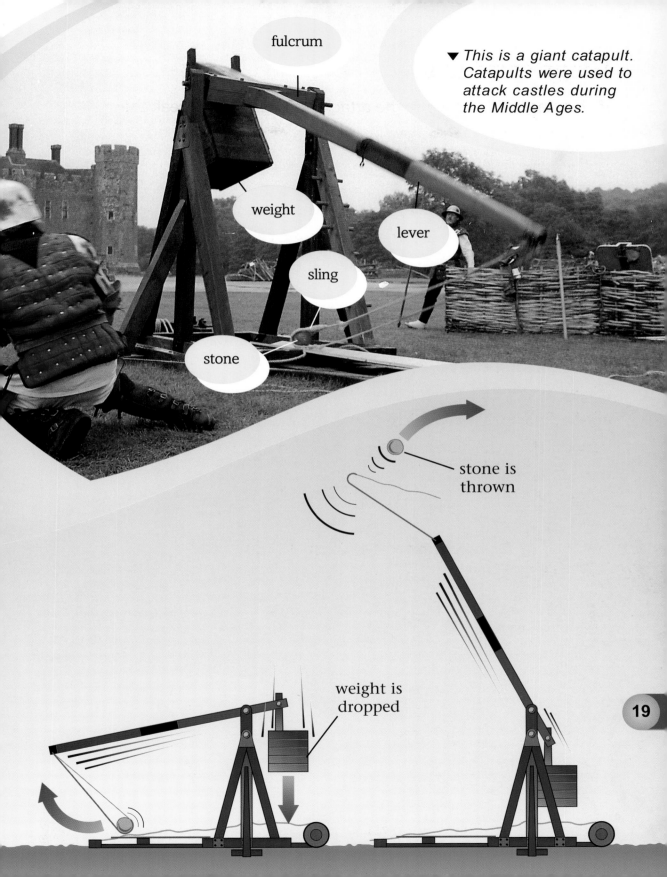

fulcrum

This is a giant catapult. Catapults were used to attack castles during the Middle Ages.

weight

lever

sling

stone

stone is thrown

weight is dropped

19

20

▲ This castle wall has fallen down in the past. Stonemasons have tried to repair it.

Digging a tunnel

If the catapults did not work, the attackers could try to dig under the castle walls. The attackers dug a tunnel. They used the tunnel to make the castle wall fall down.

The diggers used shovels to dig out the soil. They used **levers** called crowbars to dig out big stones. Wooden posts held up the roof of the tunnel.

The tunnel was dug under the walls. The diggers then put dry wood around the wooden posts. They then set fire to the dry wood.

The posts holding the tunnel roof started to burn. The tunnel started to fall down. When this happened, the castle wall above the tunnel also fell down.

Crowbars

*Crowbars are levers. You press on the handle with a small push, or **force**. The force at the other end is much bigger. However, you have to move the handle a long way. The lifting end of the crowbar moves only a short distance.*

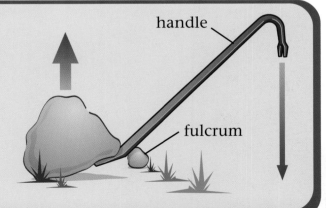

handle

fulcrum

21

force   push or pull

Clearing up

What happened when the **siege** finished? No matter who won, the castle probably needed repairs. **Stonemasons** came to mend the walls. Some stonemasons used a crane to lift the heavy stone blocks.

The stonemasons' crane was powered by a huge wheel. This wheel was called a **treadmill**. Four people walked slowly round inside the wheel to turn it.

The crane used a wheel and **axle**. The treadmill was the wheel. The axle was a thick pole called the winding drum. The rope that lifted the stone wound on to the axle.

The wheel was much bigger than the axle. So a small turning **force** on the wheel became a large force on the axle. But the wheel had to move a long way to make the axle turn a small distance.

A stonemasons' crane ▶ was used in the Middle Ages to build large stone buildings.

treadmill   large wheel that people turn by walking inside it

axle

treadmill

pulley

▼ Pulleys are still an important part of cranes today.

24

Pulleys to help the pulling

The **treadmill** crane uses small wheels. The wheels help it lift heavy weights. These wheels are called **pulleys**.

A rope threads through the two pulley wheels. One wheel is joined to the crane. The other wheel is joined to the weight. The rope has to move twice as far as it would without the pulleys. This means the stone is lifted more slowly. But the pull on the rope is only half as much as it would be without the pulleys.

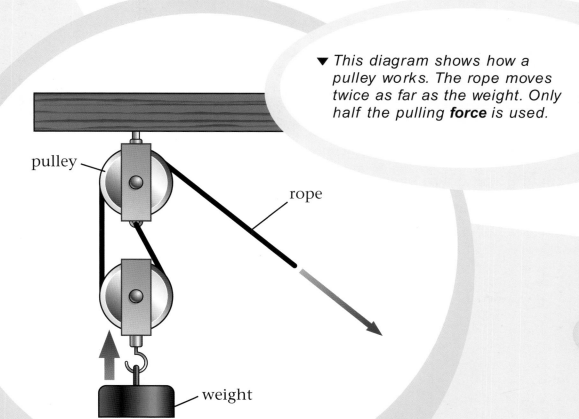

▼ This diagram shows how a pulley works. The rope moves twice as far as the weight. Only half the pulling **force** is used.

pulley

rope

weight

pulley small wheel threaded on to a rope or chain to help lift heavy weights

Built for defence

Castles were the biggest and strongest buildings in the Middle Ages. It took a long time to build a castle. It needed a lot of workers. Most work was done by hand. But the workers had **simple machines** to help them. They used wedges and ramps, for example.

A well-built castle was hard for an army to attack. Armies often had to use machines such as **siege** towers and giant catapults. Sometimes even these weapons were not enough. One answer was to wait for the people inside to run out of food and water.

Castles became easier to attack when a gun called the cannon was invented. Cannonballs could break down even the thickest stone walls. But that's another story!

Simple machines

Wedges, **ramps**, **screws**, **levers**, wheels and **axles**, and **pulleys** are all **simple machines**. They can be used to make some kinds of work easier.

Wedges

This tool uses a type of wedge. Wedges push things apart strongly when you press down. The tool is used to chop wood.

Pulleys

Pulleys are small wheels with a rope threaded through them. With two pulleys, you can lift twice as much weight with the same effort. But the rope has to be pulled twice as far.

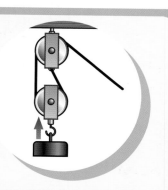

Wheels and axles

A **siege** tower and a **stonemason's** crane have wheels and axles. Moving a load on wheels is easier than dragging it.

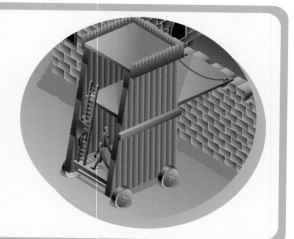

Ramps

A ramp is a slope. Pulling a heavy load up a ramp is easier than lifting it straight up. But the load has to move further.

Levers

The drawbridge, the catapult, and the crowbar are all types of lever.
A lever is a stiff bar or stick. It moves around a fixed point. This point is called the **fulcrum**.

Screws

A screw is like a ramp wound in a spiral. A crossbow uses a screw to pull back the string. With the screw, the archer can pull the string with much more **force**. But winding the string back takes much longer than just pulling it.

Glossary

archer soldier who uses a bow to fire arrows. Archers were very important before the invention of gunpowder.

axle bar with a wheel or wheels joined to it. Often there are two wheels joined to an axle, one at each end.

force push or pull. You need a force to get something moving or to make something happen.

fulcrum fixed point that a lever moves around. It is sometimes called a pivot.

knight in history, an important man who was trained to fight. Many knights lived in castles.

lever beam of some kind that can move around a single point called the fulcrum. Levers can be used to raise a castle drawbridge.

pulley small wheel threaded on to a rope or chain to help lift heavy weights. Most cranes use pulleys.

ramp flat surface that has one end higher than the other. Ramps help us move things up or down.

screw rod of wood or metal with a spiral shape around it. Screws are often used to fix things together.

siege when an army surrounds an enemy castle. The army stops food getting to the people in the castle.

simple machine tool used to push or pull something. Many simple machines were used during the Middle Ages to build castles.

stonemason person who makes things out of stone. Stonemasons used wedges to cut stones.

treadmill large wheel that people turn by walking inside it. In the past, treadmills were used to power some machines.

wedge piece of wood or metal that is thin at one end and thick at the other. The cutting edges on knives, axes, and other tools are wedge-shaped.

Want to know more?

Books

- *The Way Things Work*, David Macaulay, Neil Ardley (Dorling Kindersley, 2004).
- *Science Experiments with Simple Machines*, Sally Nankivell-Aston, Dot Jackson (Franklin Watts, 2000).

CD-ROMs

- *The New Way Things Work,* David Macaulay, Neil Ardley (Dorling Kindersley, 1998).

  If you like the book, try the CD-ROM.

Websites

- edheads.org/activities/simple-machines
  Games with simple machines and a hovering robot.

- kotn.ntu.ac.uk/castle/
  You can wander around all parts of this castle, from the dungeons to the tallest tower.

- www.castlesontheweb.com/photoarchive/index.php
  The best collection of castle photos on the internet.

- www.coe.uh.edu/archive/science/science_lessons/scienceles1/finalhome.htm
  Some experiments with simple machines.

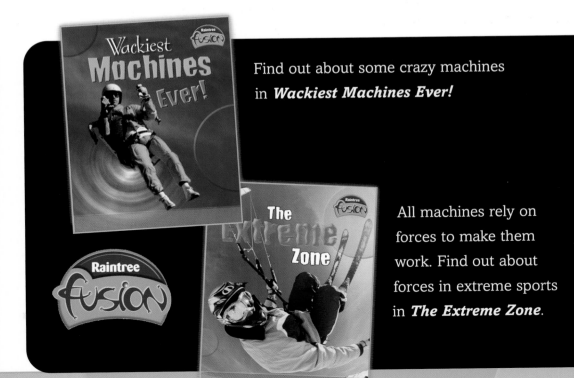

Find out about some crazy machines in *Wackiest Machines Ever!*

All machines rely on forces to make them work. Find out about forces in extreme sports in *The Extreme Zone*.

Index

Fulvio Testa

Too Much Rubbish

North-South Books · New York · London

"Tony, will you put the rubbish out?" said his mother.

"Okay," said Tony.

He picked up the big black sack and carried it downstairs.

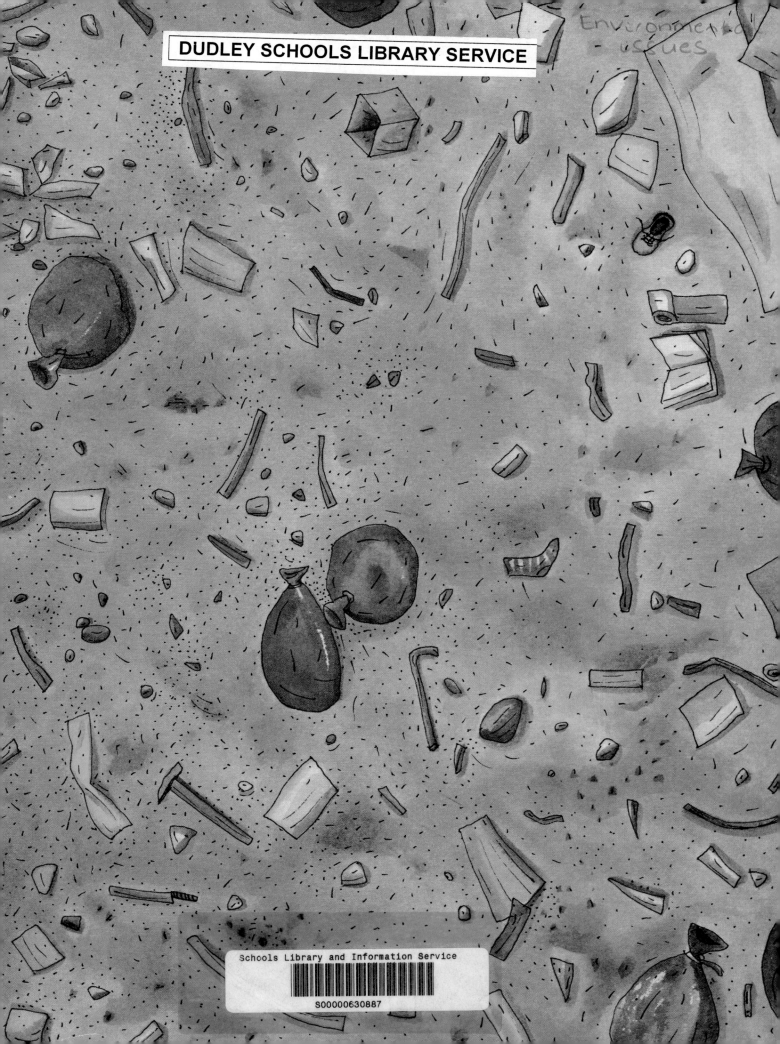

Environmental issues

Copyright © 2001 by Nord-Süd Verlag AG, Gossau Zürich, Switzerland
First published in Switzerland under the title *Ein kleines Wunder mitten im Müll*
English translation copyright © 2001 by North-South Books Inc.

First published in Great Britain, Australia, and New Zealand in 2001
by North-South Books, an imprint of Nord-Süd Verlag AG,
Gossau Zürich, Switzerland.

A CIP catalogue record for this book
is available from The British Library.
ISBN 0-7358-1453-8
1 3 5 7 9 10 8 6 4 2
Printed in Italy

For more information about our books, and the authors and artists
who create them, visit our web site: www.northsouth.com

Outside, he met his friend Bill. He had a sack of rubbish to dump at the roadside, too.

Tony and Bill set off through the town.
"Everywhere you look there's rubbish," said Bill.

"People throw stuff out of their windows," said Tony.

"They throw things out of cars."

"And one day those cars will get thrown on the scrap heap."

"There's even rubbish hanging from the trees!" said Bill.

"Look!" said Bill. "There must be a million bags of rubbish here."

"More than that," declared Tony. "A billion trillion bags of rubbish!"

"Mountains of rubbish," grumbled Bill.

"Nothing but rubbish wherever you look."

"No, Bill! Look! There's something else here!" cried Tony.

"A flower!" exclaimed Tony. "A flower right in the middle of all this rubbish!"

"It's amazing!" Bill agreed.

Tony and Bill looked at the flower for a long time.

"We need less rubbish and more flowers," said Bill finally.

"Yes, we've got to do something!" said Tony. "It's up to us."